Mia Hamm

SOCCER STAR

by
Daryl Davis Zarzycki

Mitchell Lane
PUBLISHERS

P.O. Box 196
Hockessin, Delaware 19707
Visit us on the web: www.mitchelllane.com
Comments? email us: mitchelllane@mitchelllane.com

Printing   3   4   5   6   7   8

A Robbie Reader

Freddy Adu	David Beckham	Brandi Chastain
Landon Donovan	Hilary Duff	Dale Earnhardt Jr.
Thomas Edison	Albert Einstein	Philo T. Farnsworth
Henry Ford	Robert Goddard	Johnny Gruelle
Mia Hamm	Harley-Davidson	Tony Hawk
Syd Hoff	LeBron James	Donovan McNabb
Shaquille O'Neal	Alex Rodriguez	Dr. Seuss
Charles Schulz	Josh Wolff	

Library of Congress Cataloging-in-Publication Data
Zarzycki, Daryl Davis.
      Mia Hamm: soccer star / Daryl Zarzycki.
         p. cm. — (A Robbie reader)
  Includes bibliographical references and index.
      ISBN 1-58415-286-9 (library bound)
  1. Hamm, Mia, 1972 — Juvenile literature. 2. Soccer players — United States — Biography — Juvenile literature. 3. Women soccer players — United States — Biography — Juvenile literature I. Title. II. Series.
  GV942.7.H27Z37 2005
  796.334'092 — dc22

2004009305

ABOUT THE AUTHOR: Daryl Davis Zarzycki is currently a second-grade teacher at Jennie Smith Elementary School in Newark, Delaware. She is married and has three grown children. She graduated from the University of Delaware with degrees in Elementary and Special Education. Her favorite subjects are science and math. And of course, she loves to write.

PHOTO CREDITS: Cover: Getty Images; p. 4 Getty Images; p. 6 AP Photo/ Armando Franca; p. 7 Ronald Martinez/Getty Images; p. 8 Sports Illustrated for Kids; p. 10 Barbara Marvis; p. 12 Getty Images; p. 14 AP Photo/Bob Jordan; p. 16 Rick Stewart/Getty Images; p. 18 AP Photo; p. 20 AP Photo/Chris O'Meara; p. 22 top and bottom: Getty Images; p. 23 Mia Hamm Foundation; p. 24 Jeff Gross/Getty Images; p. 26 top and bottom: Angela Rowlings/AP Photo; p. 28 Donald Miralle/Getty Images.

ACKNOWLEDGMENTS: The following story has been thoroughly researched, and to the best of our knowledge, represents a true story. While every possible effort has been made to ensure accuracy, the publisher will not assume liability for damages caused by inaccuracies in the data, and makes no warranty on the accuracy of the information contained herein. This story has not been authorized nor endorsed by Mia Hamm.

TABLE OF CONTENTS

A Robbie Reader

Mia warms up before a game. Here she is playing with the U.S. Women's National Soccer Team.

WHAT IT TAKES TO WIN

Would you like to be known as one of the world's best soccer players? If you would, Mia Hamm would tell you that it takes much practice.

When Mia was in college, her soccer coach spied her doing something special. It was very early one morning. Most people were asleep. Mia was running in the park.

Mia stretches before each game.

The coach was surprised because Mia was the best player on his team. She had more talent than anyone he had ever seen. The coach wrote Mia a letter. He told her how much he liked her hard work. She still has his letter. It says that winners are people who work their hardest when no one else is watching them.

Mia has always worked hard. Many people think Mia is the best girl soccer player ever. It is no wonder.

Here is Mia in Brazil on July 13, 2003. She plays hard in every game.

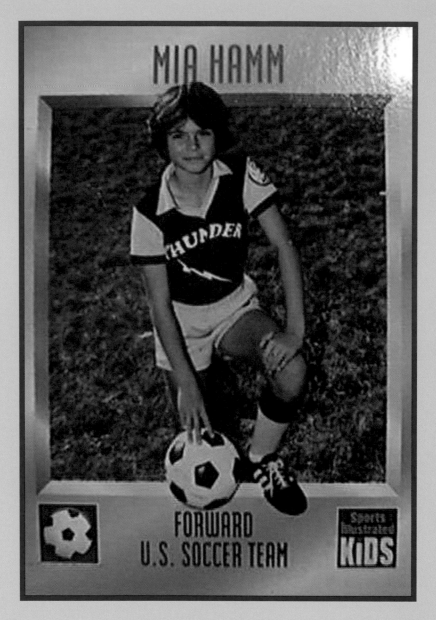

This is young Mia Hamm on the cover of *Sports Illustrated for Kids*.

LITTLE MIA

Mariel Margaret Hamm, called Mia, was born on March 17, 1972, in Selma, Alabama. She had five brothers and sisters. Their mother, Stephanie, was a dancer. Mia's father, Bill, was a colonel (KUR-n'l) in the U.S. Air Force.

Mia's family moved around a lot because of her father's job. In one way this was fun. Mia lived in many different places. In other ways it was hard. She never lived in one place long enough to make good friends.

When Mia was seven, she and her family moved to Italy. This move changed her life. In Italy, people played soccer a lot. Mia was good at sports. Soon she was playing soccer.

Many kids today enjoy playing soccer. Mia has done a lot to make soccer a popular sport for kids.

Mia's ten-year-old brother, Garrett, loved soccer also. He was a great player. Mia and Garrett were very close. She followed him around all day, and he always looked out for his sister. "Nobody wanted Mia to be on their team because she was so little," said her mother. "But Garrett always made sure that he picked her on his team."

Little Mia could run fast. She shocked everyone. She was able to beat many of the older kids to the ball.

Mia (in green) plays against Leslie Gallimore (in red). They are at the
U.S. Olympic Festival in 1989.

SOCCER STAR

As she grew, Mia enjoyed playing many sports. She was very good at football and soccer. She had to try hard because she was so small. She tried her hardest when her big brother was around. She always wanted to play with Garrett. He was so talented. She said, "I would do anything to play on his team."

When Garrett was 16, he got very sick. He had a problem with his blood, and sometimes it made him feel terrible. Mia was sad about his illness, but on days when Garrett felt better, they still enjoyed playing soccer.

By middle school, Mia and her family lived in Texas. Mia played Little League baseball. She also played on the school's football team. But

Anson Dorrance, Mia's coach for the U.S. Women's National Team.

she soon decided that she was best at soccer. She played on soccer teams and was the best player. By high school, she decided to play only soccer.

In high school, Mia became a star. During one of her games, Anson Dorrance spotted her. He was the U.S. Women's National Team coach. He asked her to join his team. She was excited. She would get to play with the best players in the United States.

The U.S. Women's National Team traveled to China. They played against the Chinese national team. Mia played well and her team won 2-0.

Mia couldn't wait to get to college. She took extra classes in high school to finish early. She graduated from high school in 1988.

Mia entered the University of North Carolina. Anson Dorrance was a coach there. Mia helped the team, called the Tar Heels, win the college championship.

Mia poses for a picture during a game against Canada in 1993. She is on the U.S. Women's National Team.

Mia finished her second year of college. She was again chosen to be on the Women's National Team. They wanted to play in the Women's World Cup, a very tough competition. Mia decided to leave college for a while to practice with her team. They practiced for a whole year.

The U.S. team made it to the world finals. They played against the team from Norway. One of Mia's teammates made a goal with only a few minutes left. They all jumped for joy! They had won. They were the champs of the world.

U.S. wins against Denmark on Sunday, July 21, 1996. The game was played in Orlando, Florida.

OLYMPIC STAR

Mia graduated from the University of North Carolina in 1994. On December 17 that year, she married Christian Corey. He was a Marine Corps pilot.

Mia and Christian moved to Florida. There Mia trained again with the Women's National Team. The team lived together and practiced every day. They were getting ready for the 1996 Olympic (O-LIM-pik) Games. They wanted to win the gold medal.

Mia cheers after she scores a goal against Denmark. This game was
played in Orlando, Florida on July 21, 1996.

Finally, July came and the Olympics began. In the first game, Mia shot two goals into the net. The U.S. beat Denmark 3-0. In the second game, Mia hurt her ankle. She couldn't play in the third. That game the U.S. tied China.

Mia played the fourth game against Norway. She was still injured but she played her best. The U.S. won the game.

Then Mia's team had to play China again. The winner would get the gold medal. The fans chanted, "U.S.A., U.S.A., U.S.A." Mia was still hurt, but she would not sit out this game. Mia was a star. She played hard and helped her teammates to score. They won 2-1. They won the gold medal!

Mia's brother Garrett was happy. He had come to see the team win. He was very sick, though. A few months after the Olympics, he died. "I have been blessed by so many things," Mia said. "But I would give back any of these victories to have Garrett's life back."

Mia visits with her fans. Kids love to get her autograph.

Mia started an organization (or-gan-ih-ZAY-shun) called the Mia Hamm Foundation. It raises money for people to study blood diseases. She wanted to help others who had the same kind of illness Garrett had. The foundation also raises money to help young athletes reach their goals.

The Mia Hamm Foundation works to raise money to study blood diseases.

Mia and Nomar together at Fenway Park on October 17, 2003.

Mia and her husband, Christian, divorced after six years of marriage. It was hard for them to make a life together because they spent so much time away from each other.

On November 22, 2003, Mia married again. Her husband is Nomar Garciaparra. He is the shortstop for the Boston Red Sox.

Mia has made the game of soccer important in the U.S. and important for women. "We are extremely lucky to be able to do what we do and play the game that we love to play," she said about women's soccer. People will remember her for all her hard work in this popular sport.

Mia receives an award on August 22, 2003.

1972	Mariel Margaret Hamm is born on March 17
1987	At 15, becomes the youngest player ever to join the National Team
1989	Attends University of North Carolina and wins her first championship
1991	Is the youngest member of the U.S. World Cup championship team
1994	Graduates from University of North Carolina; marries Christian Corey
1996	Helps U.S. team win Olympic gold medal
1997	Brother Garrett dies after long illness
1999	Member of U.S. team that wins Women's World Cup; forms the Mia Hamm Foundation
2000	Helps U.S. team win Olympic silver medal
2001	With other 1999 World Cup team players, starts WUSA, a professional women's soccer league in U.S.
2003	Marries Nomar Garciaparra
2004	Olympic Games in Athens, Greece

- All-time leading scorer in NCAA (college association) women's soccer history with 103 goals and 72 assists for a combined total of 278 points over 91 games
- Led the nation in scoring in 1990, 1992, and 1993
- Scored more goals than any other player in NCAA Division 1 history
- Registered 11 NCAA career three-goal games
- All-time leader in NCAA career assists with 72
- Set NCAA record for single-season assists with 33 in 1992
- Set NCAA record for single-season scoring with 97 points in 1992
- Holds NCAA Tournament career records for scoring (41 points), goals (16) and assists (9)
- Holds NCAA Tournament records for single-season scoring for points (16 in 1993), goals (6 in 1993) and assists (tied the record with 4 in 1993)
- World's leading goal scorer in international competition, male or female

Hamm, Mia. *Go For the Goal : A Champion's Guide to Winning in Soccer and Life.* New York: HarperCollins, 1999.

Mia Hamm Profile: "Soccer Star Raising Goals in Women's Sports." http://www.cnn.com/CNN/Programs/people/shows/hamm/profile.html

Torres, John Albert. *Mia Hamm.* A Real-Life Reader Biography. Newark, DE: Mitchell Lane Publishers, 1999.

The Mia Hamm Foundation
www.miafoundation.org

U.S. Soccer
www.ussoccer.com

Women's United Soccer Association (WUSA)
www.wusa.com